Learning How to Live Again

—The Compelling, True Story of Ryan L. Sanders

By
Ryan L. Sanders

PublishAmerica
Baltimore

ISBN: 1-60474-459-6
PUBLISHED BY PUBLISHAMERICA, LLLP
www.publishamerica.com
Baltimore

Printed in the United States of America

Thanks bro for being cool & all the great times shared together!

Ryan Danderson

The road is long, but the promise is great!

THE FALL

Chapter 1
The Sport

It was the first month of summer, and I had just joined a summer track club, no, *the* summer track club, Track Dallas. I had gotten into it with my girlfriend, her little brother, and her younger cousin. We all trained hard in the hot, hot sun for a little over a month right after the high school track season. It all came down to the Dallas conference championship meet. This meet was to see who would qualify for the national regional competition down in San Antonio that year. I ran mid-distance. The others did the same. I was entered in the 800 meter race, the 1500 meter race, and the 4 by 800m relay. You are only allowed to run in three events. Veronica, my girlfriend at the time, she was entered in all the same races as I. Her little brother was placed in the long jump, the 4 by 100m relay, and the 800m race. Veronica's cousin, Krystal Rodriguez, was put into the 1500m race, the 5000m race, and the 4 by 800m relay. She was the most talented one of all of us. She won all of her individual events: in the 5000m race her time was a 19 minute and so many seconds, the 1500m was ran by her in a time of 5 minutes and 7 seconds, and if anyone knows anything about track, she was fast or her age (15). I placed third in the 800m race with a time of 1:59, second in the 1500m, regretfully since that was my race. I worked for years training for the mile (1609 meters). But with a time of 4:28, I didn't feel too shaby. Veronica did well in her events as well, she placed third in her individual races. I'm not going to tell her times because she would probably get mad at me. And I apologize to Dylan, I have forgotten his times. I just know he placed third in both the long jump and in the 800m race, and his relay team placed second I believe.

To qualify for the regional competition in San Antonio you had to place in the top three. Thankfully, we all did right up to our last events of the day. The 4 by 800m races, they went from youngest to old. Veronica's team had both her and her cousin Krystal. They ran fairly well, placing second, only a few seconds off of the leader. Then the last 4 by 800m relay race took place, the young men's division. My team started off in a pretty good place, third, but slowly declined after that. I was chosen to be our last leg for that race which is the leg teams usually save for the best runner they have for that distance. I wasn't too excited about it when I was handed the baton in fifth place. I just had two laps to make up the slack. On the first lap I quickly caught and passed two teams, if I could just keep that place the team would make it to San Antonio. But, of course, I wanted more. I easily caught one team down the backstretch, and just had 200 meters to catch the lead team. The only problem was their last leg was 50 meters ahead of me. So, I was only able to race up to right behind him as he crossed the finish line. We placed second, more than qualifying for the regional competition.

Veronica, her younger cousin and little brother, and myself had all won medals and achieved a trip to San Antonio. Just what all of our goals had been from the beginning of the summer. We were all so happy and pleased with ourselves. If only I could have known what would happen, I wouldn't have been so overjoyed.

Chapter 2
The Crash

All of us were excited to make the trip. We were set to go a couple of days later. Veronica and I both got up thinking that we should go to the mall and shop. Yes, I'm a man who likes to shop. Not quite to the extent as women do. I like to shop for something I need or want, and I like to look pretty good. So we went to the mall. My memory is still a little fuzzy about that day. I'm not sure of which mall we went to or if we got anything. I do know her little brother, Dylan, tagged along. After we were done looking I suppose we decided not to purchase anything because I don't have anything new now, that I did not have before. Excluding all of my possessions received in the past couple of years. Then, we all loaded up in my Ford Explorer that I had for the past year and a half. I was just about to get it fixed in a few days from the small dent I had put into it a couple of months ago (it was late at night and I was tired, coming home one evening from my girlfriend, Veronica's house, I hadn't noticed that I was slowly veering off the road, and I kind of edged off the road to hit a big wooded business sign being held up by metal posts.) Anyways, back to the story. We were on our way down Lancaster Road, I was taking Veronica and Dylan home. We pulled up on Beltline and stopped at a 4-Way stop, or what I thought was a 4-way stop. I'm pretty unclear about all that happened, I'm just going by what other people have told me. So, we were stopped, there weren't any other cars stopped except for someone behind me. Therefore, I guess I thought that I had the right of way. Little did I think of the big, 5-ton gravel truck that was coming at 50 mph to intersect us. Undoubtedly, it broad-sided us, hitting the driver's side, my side. Dylan hurt his arm causing him to wear a cast for a couple of weeks, and Veronica hurt her neck which made her wear a neck-brace for a week or two. She was delusional right after the accident, walking around, freaked out from what had just happened. I, on the other hand, was pretty calm, knocked unconscious, with a traumatic brain injury as a result. Not to mention the thousands of little pieces of glass stuck in my skin, needless to say: I was having a Great, Grand Old-time! We were all rushed to the emergency room of different hospitals. It was June 27th, 2001. Veronica and Dylan's parents were worried sick about their youngsters and about me, as were my parents when they all found out. Veronica and Dylan were allowed to leave the next day. I'm not sure about Dylan, but the first thing Veronica did was to come see me and how I was doing. I was in a coma with a few cracked ribs, but nothing broken. That and my hair was cut bald because my head had some major damage done to it and they had to perform surgery on my brain. I was actually rather lucky in that all of my scars were on top of my head where my hair grew back, so I was still pretty handsome. Except for one scar down the middle of my stomach, they had to cut me open and remove my spleen. So I guess, or at least I hope, that you don't really need a spleen. At least that is what they told me. Oh, and the surgery scar gave me an excuse to show off my six-pack. That, and the fact that I didn't die also made me feel lucky, that probably would've rather sucked.

Now, while this was all happening (me being in the coma, people worrying sick about me, wondering if I'm going to wake-up, thinking I'll have serious deficits when, or if I wake up) I'm going through this elaborate, extremely long, dream state. It just kept jumping from one scene to the next, and I knew none of it was real, but I couldn't do anything about it. It was actually, rather remarkable because I just had decided that if this next scene wasn't real I would kill myself because it was making me crazy. The remarkable thing was that right then, at that point in the dream, it was real life! And once I found this out, it made me so glad. I had woken up! It only took two months! Oh, by the way, I was being sarcastic. Everyone was so happy to see me up that they notified everyone who knew about the incident. They were all happy, I was happy, we all rejoiced praising, "God is good!"

Chapter 3
The Love of My Youth

Later, I found that I was in Baylor Department of Rehabilitation. First, I had been cared for by Charlton Central Hospital, they're the ones who sewed me back together, but not without taking a little souvenir to remember me by (my spleen). Next, I was taken to Life Care Hospital, it's kind of like Baylor Depart. of Rehabilitation, just that it deals with victims that have had some type of injury during the early stages of their "getting back to normal stage," as I prefer to call it. And finally, I was transferred to Baylor Rehab., which resided in downtown Dallas, TX.

All I remember about the first few weeks is that some person wearing blue, or green, or white with little green pock-a-dotted pajamas kept coming into my room and either bringing me a tray of food or taking me to some room with a machine to test my reflexes, vision, hearing, the feeling I had on all parts of my body, comprehension of problems and situations, etc. I learned that I was very fortunate in fact. Most people would be seriously impaired, or have no hope of ever regaining normalcy, or in most cases, never even have survived a blow like that. It's a good thing I have titanium for bones, my message to all the youngsters out there, "drink milk."

Placed in little white pajamas of my own, and in a wheel chair that I had to use to roll around in, I felt like a sad patient, and I was. There was someone wearing blue, or green, or white with little green pock-a-dotted pajamas taking me to several therapies. First, it was usually the pool on the first floor, where I worked on walking and hand movement. I walked around in circles moving around my arms, and then I did some type of leg exercise. It was sad, knowing that I had been reduced to this, much of the things that I was to do were things I either had extreme difficulty doing, or couldn't even do at all, things that I used to be able to do without a problem. Very sad, but I never let it get me down. I've been complimented so many times on how positive and determined I remained, you would think I'm getting tired of it. But I'm not, I like the attention, I guess. I mean, look at all of this crap that had happened to me: I don't walk or talk correctly, I couldn't remember short-term things, I couldn't write legibly at all, and my vision was off. So, I don't mind the compliments I'm getting. It's kind of a pick-me-up.

After the pool therapy for about 30 minutes, I changed and got ready for my next therapy, Speech. I had 3 Speech therapists all together, but not all at once. I'd have one for a little while, but then they would leave Baylor Rehab. and go somewhere else. I was beginning to think it was I who was turning them all away. But then, my third Speech therapist told me that I was smart, funny, and adorable, and assured me they all couldn't have left because of me, I was too cute, as she put it. (Permission to throw up)

Then I was taken to occupational therapy, and later physical therapy. My OT, occupational therapist, was a lovely lady named Karla. She worked hard with me on problem-solving, hand coordination, and stretching. And, when it came time for physical therapy, I was most delighted. I had the pleasure of seeing a young woman named Sarah, probably the most beautiful girl there, at Baylor Rehab. She was my PT. We worked on just using a walker, instead of a wheel-chair. She was 24 years old, if my memory serves me correctly. A little old for me, since I was only 17 at the time. I was a little displeased about not being able to get a relationship started, but not for long. Somebody then mentioned Veronica to me and I was astonished, "Oh yeah! Veronica!

How is she? Is she alive?" I could not believe that I had forgotten her! My mother told me she was all right and her brother, Dylan, too. I was so relieved. She and Dylan were both back in school and doing just fine. As soon as they put a phone in my room, I called her. She was so happy to hear my voice, and was wondering how I was doing.

I instantly forgot about Sarah. From then on I thought everything would be okay. I wanted to see Veronica as soon as I heard her sweet voice. I later learned that her and her whole immediate family had been there every day while I was in a coma to see how I was doing. They set up a time to come see me that week, and man, was I excited!

Chapter 4
What's with Hospitals?

Sarah ended up leaving Baylor as well, she went to Michigan to sculpt ice statues, I guess. No, not really. She went there for a bigger job offer I think. But I didn't really care, because I was going to get to see my princess the very next day. Veronica and her family happily came the next afternoon. They all said hello and asked how I was doing with such enthusiasm. All I could do was stare at Veronica. She leaned in to give me a hug smiling, with that beautiful smile that I remembered. They were all talking to me, but I didn't really hear them very much. All of my attention was focused on my beautiful love, Veronica. She sat next to me and everyone else stood around somewhere. We all talked about the accident, what happened and how it happened. It was all new information to me, my memory had been swiped clean of that whole day, or that whole week in fact. They asked me how I felt. I sat there with my arm around Veronica, and smiled, "I feel fine now, just fine."

We were all excited about me coming home soon. My discharge date was set for September 25th, the same date as Veronica's and my two-year anniversary. About a month away from the time. I couldn't wait! I had been lying in a hospital bed for longer than two months. Oh, now I have nothing against hospitals. They're good and they help you.

But, there's something about being in an unfamiliar environment for so long. All of the nurses and doctors just smile at you with their big, white teeth. And all the other patients just stare at you, looking miserable the way their mouth frowns and they usually stare down at the floor just thinking of what their life has become. And the smell, WOOO-WEEE! It smells like my Grandmother's bathroom smells after not having been cleaned for months, and my Grand Pa's a big man. You know that old country song, "Big, bad Leeroy Brown?" Well, I think that song was about him. So obviously, I was ready to leave. I even thought about escaping a few times, but I thought I would probably hurt myself further. It was mainly the nurses that made me want to escape. They put me in one of those veil beds that they zip you up in so that you can't get out. There was this little remote in the bed so that you could call the nurses if you needed assistance. Somehow after the accident my bladder shrunk. I used to have to use the restroom only about 3 to 4 times a day. Well, now it was like once every 30 minutes. So I was calling the nurse station all the time for one of them to come unzip the bed because I had to go. After a short time, they would start taking forever. One time, I waited a little over an hour for someone to come unzip me. I kept calling, and they just said, "Yes…. someone is on their way." Like, every time I called, and I called a lot of times. Up to a point, they stopped answering me, I would press the button to call the nurse station, and they would press the button, just to show that they had answered my call. They had to do that or they could be fired. But then, not even say anything. I was so ticked off at that point, I started cursing, I said, "You better ****ing answer me ****it!" They didn't say a word. I started threatening them, "If someone doesn't come soon, I'll go on the floor!" I still got no response. I then said, "All right, you think I'm bluffing, don't you?!" Now, I've always been a man of my word, and I was extremely angry that no one had come to help me. So, well, you know what happened. I helped them clean the floor, so to speak. It didn't smell very much like pine trees, but I was giving my part back to society none-the-less. When it got closer to my release date, a doctor came to talk with my stepfather and me. He told us that since we were planning for me to return to school in the spring, I should probably

18

remain there until October 3rd and start the Day Treatment program until the end of the year. I really didn't want to, but we went ahead and took the professional doctor's recommendation, my stepfather always took Mr. PHD's opinion over mine. It was only a week longer in the hospital, but to me, it felt like a year. I then said, "maybe using the restroom on the floor wasn't such a hot idea."

I started preparing for my two-year anniversary with Veronica. I got her a silver ring, which she preferred to gold, with a beautiful purple stone. I waited to give it to her until we ate at the Olive Garden for dinner, it was our favorite restaurant. She was so delighted when she saw it. She hugged me, and then handed me my present. It was a silver, which I also preferred to gold, cross-country necklace with the sport's symbol as the emblem. I completely loved it. Cross-country being the sport where we met. I never imagined the little freshman that had a crush on me my sophomore year, was the person I would grow to love so much. We embraced and kissed, I knew she would be the one I would share many meals with pretty soon. I didn't used to feel this strongly for her, but the love she had shown by being by my side at every time she could waiting for me to wake up from my coma made me realize how special she and our connection together was.

So, the day finally came for me to leave Baylor Rehab. At that point I thought to myself that maybe it was good that I stayed a little while longer in the hospital. I mean, I was a little older, and a little taller. I'm being funny again. Sorry, I just tend to make comments like that when I'm talking about good old Baylor Rehab. Anyways, I finally went home! Do you know what the feeling of home feels like when you haven't been there for a while? Well, it felt like that.

Chapter 5
The Break-Up

Ah, home, I had been away for nearly four months. I know that to teenagers it feels really good getting away from the house every once in a while, but considering where I had been, let's just say it felt good to walk into MY room and not see a big veil bed with a sink right next to it. I was home! Finally, finally, home! I was very pleased to just lay down in MY bed and listen to my stereo. I could just stay in my room for the rest of my life, it was that peaceful. Sure, I would start to stink after a few days and probably die of starvation, but it's nice to know that you have options.

I was pretty solemn when the district meet for cross-country season came around. I couldn't even walk yet. I went to watch Veronica's district cross-country meet, like a "good little boyfriend." No, I wanted to go. Even though I was delayed from running for a while, I still loved the sport. Running was life to me, and I was interested to see how Veronica would do as well. Her goal was to make it to the regional competition in Arlington, TX. She tried really hard, but was suffering from cramps. As I'm sure you girls know, they can be quite painful. She ended up in 14th place. You have to be in the top ten to qualify for the regional competition in cross-country. She almost made it. Upset that she hadn't qualified, looking very angry, I rolled up to her in my wheel chair. I gave her a kind of half-hug, I didn't really want to give her a whole hug because well, it was a two-mile hard run and I kind of wanted to stay dry and smelling zest fully clean. So, I told her to keep her head up and that she still had next year. That's what most people say if you're not a senior and everyone knows, that's just what you say, so it makes you feel like just two bucks. And for that, I apologize to my princess. Sorry sweetie. We had lunch with both of our families after the meet. Veronica was looking depressed, so I said, "Look how many girls you did beat, it was probably 50 or more. They all have to feel a little worse than you do." She looked at me and said, "I don't really care." She might have acted like she didn't care, but I knew she did. So, I hugged her for a really long time, trying to male-nurse and console her. We made plans to meet at the Duncanville District meet the very next day. Duncanville's where I went to High School and where Veronica went to school until the end of her freshman year. That's when her parents moved her from being about 5 minutes away from me, and took her to live about 25 to 30 minutes away from me in a town called Red Oak. It was nothing against me, *they said*. No, it really wasn't, they had been planning to move for a while. It just made it a little tougher for me to see my sweet beauty.

So we met at my school's district meet the next day. I, having placed in the top ten the year prior and gaining a trip to the regional competition in Lubbock, was pretty down as I watched the races run by hundreds of other people, knowing I would've been my district's best performer that year. The only thing that perked me up was when my coach, and all of my teammates started talking about me and how good I had been. I was the #1 runner for my team for the past two years. In fact, I led the team to regionals the last year. As a team, you have to place in the top 3 to make it to the regional competition. With me leading the way and everyone else not too far behind, we had gained a trip to regionals that year. Without me and my best friend, Jason Ortiz, who had been a senior and placed 2nd for the team not too far behind me that past year, the team placed 7th out of 8 teams.

I have to admit I was a little cocky towards some of the top district runners that day. I told them that I would be ready for track season when it came in the spring. They said that it would be good to run with me again. And I told them that they might not think so after we raced. "You're good, but don't be surprised when you don't see me running along side of you, I'll probably be in the front. You might not think it's going to be good to be running against me," I said giggling. I feel kind of bad, I was pretty arrogant.

I still felt bad when my birthday came around and I had just barely started using the walker everywhere I went. It was December 7th, 2001, I had just turned 18. My parents gave me money, clothes, and other apparel items. I've forgotten what Veronica had gotten me, I think it was money. Mostly, all I remember was our break-up just a week later.

Yeah, I said break-up. Everything was fine until after our anniversary. She had asked me if there was anything else I would have rather wanted. I said, "Well, maybe a track foot instead of the cross-county emblem." But, I loved my present anyway. So then, I asked her if there was something she would've rather preferred, which I thought was why she asked me. So she could tell me what she would've rather wanted if she got to choose. Then she said, "Well, I like the ring idea, but a big diamond as the stone would've been better." So, thinking quickly I told her, "In time," to avoid any conflict that may have risen. Only, in the back of my mind I was thinking, "HOLY SH**," I couldn't believe she was expecting that. Now, not to say I didn't want to ask her, because I did. I just wanted to earn the money myself. Seeing how I had no means of income, I had decided to wait until I could work to start saving. But now, I was telling myself, "Well, since she's expecting things, I'll give her something she doesn't expect." But I didn't want to break-up with her because I've always had bad break-ups in the past. One girl threatened to kill herself over me. So, I got this stupid idea, of which I seriously regret now. I was going to make her break up with me, by cheating on her. I know I sound really horrible now. I called an old friend of mine that I dated in the eighth grade. Her name was Deanne, she was one year older than me and I asked her to come over to watch a movie. I let Veronica find out, which I thought was good at the time, my plan had worked. So anyways, Veronica drives over to my house in her truck, and gives me all my stuff back that she could find in her room, then, not undoubtedly, asks for all of her stuff. She cried and said some harsh things that I won't repeat, because it would make her seem like a cruel person, and she's not. She later told me she did not mean those things she had said, and that she was just so furious at me for doing what I had done. Then I told her that I was sorry. And man, am I extremely sorry now, for the pain that I caused her. Now, I really, really, want her back. I cannot believe that I let a very beautiful young woman who loved me more than you could ever know get away like that. Very, very stupid on my part.

Of course, time goes on, wounds heal, and you have to get ready for what comes next in life. I took some at home classes to make up for the time that I had missed in school that semester. I passed all of them and was ready to start back to the high school in January for the rest of my senior year.

Chapter 6
Back to School

January 7th, 2002, my first day back to school. Everyone was excited to see me. They all told me that they had been praying for me and they will continue to do so. I had gotten a lot of that. Everyone always tells me that they were praying for me. I think because so many people prayed, God just finally said, "Alright, alright, I'll save him. Just leave me alone." Everyone was happy to see me up and about, and in turn, I was happy to see *some* of them as well. Just kidding, I was happy to see everyone. My counselor had enrolled me in 6 courses. I had late arrival on both days. English, Office Aid, and Track on A days. Psychology, Economics, and Track again on B days. We had block scheduling, which I like because you don't have to go to the same class and see the same wrinkly, old teacher everyday. Now, there are some exceptions. Not every teacher looks old and wrinkly, just most of them.

I found it difficult for me to write when I walked into English that morning. My right hand shook, and still shakes. When I would eat, I got food all over my face. When I would brush my teeth, I'd get toothpaste in my eye. Anything and everything was just too hard for me to control with my right hand. And I was right-handed. So, I had to start using my left hand for almost everything. Eating, writing, brushing teeth, brushing hair, etc. And now, I'm fairly good with the left hand. It still takes a while to write even my name down, but it's getting better. I was always ready for track class. All of the guys told me I was an inspiration. And I told them that even though I might not be running with them, my heart and spirit would be.

When the athletes would be running out there on the track, I would always tell them to work harder, run faster, and I would advise them on race strategies and training techniques. I did what I could, everyday I was there. I would have to go back to therapy three days a week. Monday, Wednesday, and Friday for physical, occupational, and speech therapies. I really wanted and still want to drive again. I said that I wanted to have a car and be driving by graduation.

So, the people of Baylor set me up in the back-to-driving program. First there was a reaction time test, which I passed with flying colors. Who thought of that saying anyway. Probably the same person who thought of, "If pigs could fly," and, "worms with ears." I don't know about you, but I'd be pretty freaked out if I saw a pig flying and ears on a worm. But anyways, then I had to take this driving program on the computer. It's kind of like a simulated driving route that gets harder as you progress to different levels. I didn't enjoy that game too much. You had to go like, 15 miles an hour, and stop at probably 30 stop lights for each level. And as I progressed, the levels kept getting longer, and longer, and longer. Level 15 took 45 minutes! 45 minutes of just sitting there, turning out of the way of small hazards and other cars every once in a while, stopping at every stop light, every stop-sign, and every railroad crossing. It's like every traffic light, every train, and every car going the opposite way just sat there and waited for you to go by. Then they would make their move, and make you wait EVEN LONGER for the level to end.

Time went by quickly. It was March and I was now able to walk free of any device. My therapist didn't give me permission to walk without the walker yet though. So I would take the walker to school and hide it in the counselor's center, then pick it up when I headed to the stadium, which is where I was picked up everyday. I was cool with everyone that worked in the counselor's center, so they kept quiet about it. And my track coach and teammates admired me so much, they actually encouraged me to get off the walker and to stay off. So you know they weren't saying anything. My mother and stepfather didn't know that I was going against my therapist's wishes for a while. One of my friends slipped up after that. See, my parents and his parents are friends. And he told his mom that I was no longer on the walker in school. So then, his mother of course talked to my mother, and she confronted me about it. I decided to use a technique that I had never used before, the truth. Well, somewhat. I told her that yes, I was putting the walker in the counseling center for most of the day, but that I was taking it with me everyday to track practice. And that was true, I just neglected to mention the fact that taking it with me, meant that I was just carrying it along side me and not actually using it to help my balance.

It was a good thing that after a balance test a few days later, my physical therapist finally said that I had scored high enough to lose the walker for good. The test dealt with many challenging things if you had poor balance. You have to score a 45 or higher to lose a walker. I had scored just that. As soon as I did it, I really wanted to work on getting back to running even though it wasn't recommended. It was around the first of May now, summer track was going to start up again in less than one month. I wanted to get ready for it so, I asked a fellow distance runner on my team to run with me and watch, in case I were to lose my balance and fall. I was like a mentor and leader to him and everyone else on the team, so he eagerly agreed. I haven't fallen once every time that I've run! I'm just really wobbly, my hips shake uncontrollably and my legs jolt to the ground with every stride I make. So for right now I cannot run competitively, but I'm going to keep working on it. I'm never going to give up. Classmates and teammates saw this, so they voted me to be the annual receiver of the Jason Boles award.

Chapter 7
End of an Era

Before I talk about the Jason Boles award, I'll talk about prom. Since Veronica and I were no longer together, I started looking for a date. Came across one girl in my psychology class who was very nice and sweet to me, and looked like she would fit well in a prom dress. Her name was Brooke Johnson, she was a junior. She told me that she would love to go with me, so I rented the tux, ordered the limo, got her a corsage, and made dinner reservations at a little Italian place, called Lombardi's that resided in Downtown Dallas. Only a few minutes away from the Apparel Mart, which is where the event was held. Oh, and after I had asked her, I kind of found out her little nickname that everyone knew about, except me. The nickname was "Bubbly Brooke," I need not explain. But anyways, my tux looked good, it was black, with a shiny royal blue vest underneath the jacket. That and I was wearing some half-swayed, half-dressy (shiny) black shoes. Brooke looked phenomenal. She had a shiny, lavender, tight dress on. It looked just magnificent. When I commented on how beautiful she looked, she tried to be modest and said that I looked great. So we, of course, took pictures of us, our families, and of us leaving to go to the restaurant. You know, for the parents. They always have to take pictures of every single semi-important event. Your first step, your first lost tooth, the first time you use the restroom by yourself, etc.

When we finally made it to the restaurant, we saw some friends of mine. We shook hands, told each other how nice each of us looked, in a manly fashion of course, and said how great each of our dates looked. They kind of asked me why I had decided to take "Bubbly Brooke." All I could say was that I hadn't prior learned of her nickname. Of course, no one believed me when I said that because supposedly, everyone knew. So, whatever, we all know how immature assumptions can be made about people, especially in high school. I can assure you, she's a very nice, sweet, and gorgeous young woman. Maybe not the sharpest knife in the drawer, but she sure did look beautiful that night. We didn't end up arriving to prom until about 9:30 that night of April 20th, 2002, but it lasted until 12 in the morning. All we missed out on was the food prepared for all of us. We ate dinner before we went there because, well basically, I like my elbow room.

So, when we got there, we had to take pictures. Because there can never be enough pictures. It took about a half an hour to wait in line just to stand there and take one shot. I'm glad that I spent $40 on prom pictures. You work hard for the money so that you can look good and you get up there to take just one shot, then quickly move out of the way so that you don't hold up the line. It was such a rewarding memory. I look stupid, of course. Yeah, really, really happy I did that!

Then we danced. It was pretty cool, they had all the current hit songs playing. I mostly walked around and talked to all of my friends. Everyone wanted to take pictures with me, and in turn, I wanted to take pictures with some of them. Then, my date and I took a few pictures of us with my disposable camera that my mother was sure to get me. I danced a few times, and had a lot of fun. That was actually, a wonderful senior moment.

At the end of the dancing, we got back into the limo and drove to pick up one of my date's friends. One of her female friends no doubt, or else I wouldn't have agreed. We drove around for a while, until we got to Brooke's friend's grandmother's house, then they were dropped off. I called some friends of mine and saw where all of the after prom parties were at. Right around 2 a.m., I finally went home. My driver was only paid for until midnight. But, because he was such a cool, older guy, he gave me an extra couple free hours. The night eventually, came to a close.

Prom was talked about for weeks to come. I'm still hearing about it now in fact. It was being talked about during the honors night assembly, which was held during the middle of May. I was invited by the school there. The only funny thing about that night was when we stood up and cited the pledge of allegiance. They had an army guy hold up this big flag with a long wooden pole. He held the pole to the crowd, but it was apparently heavy. So, he helped it being held with his crouch. So he had this extremely long wooden pole sticking out from his crouch. A couple friends of mine and myself just started cracking up, laughing. Because, well, you know what it looked like. Sporting wood, when it's not literal it can be embarrassingly funny.

The Jason Boles award was one of the first awards presented. It recognizes a DHS student who has overcome some medical adversity to make a significant contribution to Panther athletics. Oh, by the way, my school's team mascot are the panthers. Go Panthers! I was nervous and sweating. I really, really, really wanted to win this award. When they pulled the name out of the little envelope, I was holding my breath. I was so tense, I felt like having a heart attack right there. But then, they named Ryan Sanders as the recipient. I would have been so disappointed if they didn't pick me. Mostly because they had told me that I was going to receive the award, and that would have been a cruel joke. I was the only one to get a standing ovation from all of the students. It made me happy to know that everyone appreciated me and everything I had accomplished.

After that, I was ready to graduate. A couple of days before graduation, all the seniors got a chance to strut their stuff at Senior Showcase, a formal occasion where all of the seniors that want to, walk across a stage and get two of their high school accomplishments read aloud to the audience. I asked to escort my mother, which is what several other seniors decided to do. I thought it was just another excuse to take more pictures. There were many seniors who decided to do this. We have over 650 students in my class, and my last name is Sanders. So, my mother and I were in for a long wait. But after everyone was called, and after we took the PICTURES, it was finally our turn. As soon as they called my name, Ryan Sanders, everyone whooped and hollered, it was crazy. I got such loud applause, I couldn't hear my accomplishments being read. But they were as follows: #1, Ryan has been a member of the Spanish National Honors Society for two years, and #2, Ryan was the lead runner for cross-country and mid to long distance track for two years. I had to bust out with a smile and giggle as I walked down the stage with everybody yelling for me. As I walked back to my seat, everyone told me, "Good job Ryan."

It was just two days before graduation. Everyone else and myself couldn't wait to receive our diplomas! When the day finally came, just about everyone was nervous of looking like a fool walking across the stage. I just hoped I didn't lose my balance and fall on my face. But I'm a pretty confident person so I wasn't worried. Since everyone else was nervous, naturally, most people forgot something they were supposed to wear, like a sash, medal, the, "I'm with stupid" graduation robe, etc. But everything came out just fine. Everyone who graduated got their diplomas, the wait was long, but expected to be so, and the ceremony was pulled off with very few hitches.

When it was my turn to walk across the stage, I tried to think of something to do that would set me apart from the rest. So I got this cool idea to hold my arm in the air and to make a #1 sign with my hand. I thought since I had been through so much recently, everyone would be accepting of me doing so and not think I was too arrogant. Or at least, I hoped. Well, when they called my name everyone stood up immediately, clapping and yelling praise for what I had done. It made me feel pretty confident walking across the stage to get my diploma. I was overjoyed to be the only one to receive a standing ovation at graduation. Well besides the very last person of course, Angela Zett. She was loved by many fellow classmates, including myself. That and we were so happy to finally reach the end of the 756 name list. We had done it! Reached the end of the twelve year journey, or hell as I like to refer to it.

Chapter 8
The Realization

After graduation there were several parties, and pictures no doubt. This time it was actually a mutual thing. It was for the parents like always, but also for us now. Well, some that is. So we could remember this joyful mark in time of the end of such a big part of our lives. Therefore, it was also party time. We had lots of fun, doing stuff to each other we probably wouldn't have done unless we knew it would be a long time before we saw each other again. I remember that I told a lot of girls I had always liked them. And I had, but I would never have told them that before because the word would have eventually gotten around to Veronica, but I had broken up with her. So I went to a couple parties, had one myself actually. It was all a good time. There was always someone drinking, which wasn't too out of the ordinary. I know it was wrong, I just told myself that everyone did this. And most people did. I didn't drink that much, but I didn't stop anyone else from doing so either. When the parties came to an end, we all shook hands, hugged the girls, and some got ready to leave for college, the armed forces, or just getting the hell out of Duncanville. I was going to travel to Washington D.C. where my uncle and his family lived. But it wasn't until later that June. So I had some free time. When I went to church on Sunday, oh yeah, I went to church semi-regularly. I guess I haven't really mentioned that, and I probably wouldn't have until now. You see, I started writing this book at the end of my senior year. But I didn't pay much attention to God until early that June.

I was in the youth Sunday-school class and they mentioned the summer retreat that they had every year. It was going to be held in the middle of June at a campsite in Texas, about an hour drive away from the church which resided in Midlothian, Texas. I always passed on the church—class trips because of work, or athletics, but I never really cared to go either. Well I knew I wouldn't be able to race for any medals for a while. I wasn't in summer track this year for obvious reasons. And I didn't want to sit on the sidelines rooting for my team because it would make me feel just too bad. Thinking of what I could've been. I was so sad. But I thought, "God saved me for a reason, I should find out what that is." I had been straying away from His word, the Christian life, for too long. I knew He was my One and only Savior. But I indulged myself in the pleasures of this world for most of my life, only giving Him praise on certain Sundays when I felt like going or when I didn't want to be looked down on by my family for not attending church.

What was once doing it because I had nothing better to do became the greatest experience of my life.

THE RISE

Chapter 9
Camp

S o the day came for us to pile into cars, trucks, vans, and other vehicles that I'm sure were used in the biblical times. I was on this trip to find out something that God put in my heart. But as I didn't know the truth or didn't see the true light yet, I was of course, checking the vehicles to find the most attractive group to ride with because well, you know. I came across the Molleur's family van. The two daughters, Tara and Aryn, were 18 and 16, and two of the best looking girls there. Erin brought along a friend of hers who was very cute as well. There mom was really nice and she was the driver. The young son, Jonus, was going also, whom I didn't really know that well, but he turned out to be a pretty cool little dude. I think someone else rode in the passenger seat up front, but I cannot remember who that was. It was about a 3 or 4-hour drive, and all those bottles that came down off the wall were starting to really annoy me. No, I'm just kidding. We did have fun talking, joking, and laughing most of the way there.

When we arrived, I was surprised that the camp would be as open as it was. There were about 20 smaller houses that were set up for other church groups and our group to reside in during our stay. We first stopped at the girl's house to unpack their things. There were many nice, cute young ladies from our church, so I, still being girl crazy, offered my help. When I walked into their room, I picked out a bed, went to it, then said, "All right, I've got mine picked out." We all had a good laugh, and to my dismay, they told me that the boys had a separate room. So I sadly picked up my big feet, and followed the other guys into our room. It was so small, there were about twenty some odd guys, so we didn't unpack our things because we knew how easily they could be, "misplaced," in such a tiny room. Not to say that we all weren't trustworthy, but come on, you wouldn't want to lay a fifty-dollar bill in the middle of twenty out-of-work, young kids would you. We were all either friends, or became friends at the church camp. But still, it's the principle of the matter.

All those worries faded away when it came time to meet in the Tabernacle for our first worship session of the camp. The band was great, everyone rejoiced in beautiful worship songs for our Creator and His Son. I really liked it, probably more than I ever had. At the end of the song session by (band name), the speaker of the camp, David Nasser, opened with his own powerful testimony. Then he branched out amazing lessons from his story and it all rang true in my heart. So when he asked if anyone had a desire to either accept Jesus Christ as their own personal savior, or maybe reclaim His name at the head of their life, I raised my hand as we were all told to close our eyes and think of our lives. I knew I had been running wild for so long, not completely knowing of the truth. On the very first day, our awesome speaker, David Nasser's very first speech of the camp, I realized what had been missing for so long, and rededicated my life to the King, our God Almighty. David then prayed with all of us. There were more than fifty kids who either dedicated or rededicated their lives to the Christ on the very first night of the camp. There were over 200 in all that week, truly amazing.

It was so glorious to see what God had done. And know that His work will continue to touch so many lives. Until the day this world falls and we are sent to be with Him, He will make so many people that haven't seen the Light, feel such joy. Become full of His hope, His peace, His love. Forever and ever.

The following days were spiritual and fun. There were many games that we played in teams, wonderful fellowship. We had a real "Hee-hah" time, and I don't just mean the rednecks. As our time came to an end, I left with a new hope for my life. And a new mission to forever walk with the Lord.

Chapter 10
New Life

When I returned home, I was so excited to tell the story. I wanted everyone to know about it. My friends and family were so happy for me, it was really great. The youth department at church was asked to tell the whole congregation of our time and triumphs at camp. I had to go to Washington D.C. right away when I got back to see my Uncle Mike and his family. It was fun and very beautiful. There were a lot of sites to see. Great notes for American history. But I had already taken that class my junior year in high school, so what was the point? No, I'm kidding of course. I'm glad I had the chance to see all the historic buildings and land sites that I did. However I was more excited to get back to my church in Ovilla, Texas to spread the awesome news. So when I finally made it home for a few days, I asked the pastor, Herb Pederson, if I could give my testimony in the later church service, which more people went to at the time. He told me he was very happy the Lord had entered my life again, and that it would be great if I could share my testimony with the congregation. That made me happy and I started writing out what I was going to say. There was no nervousness when I wrote, the words just came to me as if they had been dying to break free from my sinful hands for so long. When the glorious Sunday rolled around, I was ready to go.

The church was packed that week with current members and many visitors, which is what I wanted. I wanted to open the hearts of all kinds of people and share the awesome news of Christ unto all. When they called me up, I got up and walked to the front of the service with that kind of, wobbly walk I have. I try to walk normal, but I can't because of my balance problem. And my speech is still slurred a little bit from the accident. So when I got to the front my first line was, "Now don't worry, don't worry. I'm not as think as you all drunk I am." The place overflowed with laughter. But I kept a straight face with a puzzled expression. I then said, "What? I'm really not." They continued laughing for a few moments. After I said that I was kidding and we all settled down (it didn't take too long), I gave my testimony and had it mostly memorized. If you would like to see, here it is, and if not, then I don't really care:

(Joking, of course)

Ryan's Testimony
(opening line)

My name is Ryan Sanders and I was born in December of 1983. I was blessed with a cunning mind, I would like to say pretty good physical features, and athletic abilities. Everything came fairly easy for me: school, friends, sports, relationships, etc. Something almost always happened even to where my appearance or the way other people perceived me would shine, it hardly ever faltered, I was thought to be a truly blessed boy, and that great things were to come. In fact, I'd heard these reflected appraisals, or compliments, my entire life. So it made me a little cocky starting around the age of five or six. I also came across running my freshmen year in high school. I did pretty well in track and cross-country. I could run a mile in about 4 minutes and 30 seconds. Everything in my life was going great: I had a steady girlfriend for over 2 years and we were supposedly in love, or puppy love as I like to call it. I got a car for my 16th birthday, shortly after I got a job-it might have only paid minimum wage, but that's about all you can hope for when you're 16 and just starting out in the wonderful world of fast food. And on top of it all, I was kicking butt in my athletics.

It was all just gravy until June 27th of 2001. I was taking my girlfriend and her little brother home from shopping, I think. I pulled up to a stop sign, stopped, and when I went, one of those huge gravel trucks broad-sided me traveling about 50 mph. The passengers were just fine after a week or so with a sprained arm and a slight, neck injury. The truck hit me on my side with about 20,000 lbs. of pressure. But I was okay, I mean I survived, obviously. It's a good thing I drank milk all my life, it must have given me titanium for bones. I cracked a few ribs, but not one broken bone. Anyways, I was laid up in the hospital placed into a coma for over two months. The doctors weren't sure how much of a recovery I would make, or if I would even recover at all for that matter. Some people thought I was just trying to get out of lawn mowing cause I didn't like that too much. Well, I think it's been long enough so I can tell you, they were a little-bit right. No, no, I'm just kidding. Actually after I woke up, I looked at those people and after hearing what they had said, I just grinned at them and kind of laughed, just to tease them though. It's about all the fun I could have at the time, I was pretty helpless for a while. I had completely lost my balance, which is why we're able to walk without falling, I lost my short-term memory, and I lost my short-term memory (pause for laughter), and my kind of cool voice. But I did gain one physical thing out of it. It's called ataxia, a line of tremors that stretch all up and down my right side, causing my right hand, arm, and right leg to shake uncontrollably whenever I try and concentrate on doing something with them.

So everything had been stripped away from me. I was incapable of walking, let alone running. Which was at that time, everything to me. All my goals, hopes, and dreams lied in that. I lost all of my back-up plans as well, eventually. So I was pretty down. I prayed to God everyday, asking if He could help me. I heard that so many people had prayed for me and I think God just said, "Okay, I'll save him, just stop nagging me!" No, but He did fill me with the courage and the will to push through. It took several months, but I finally got back on my feet again. I thank Him so much for that. My life is already indebted to Him for His great sacrifice to all of us, and then to save me yet again. I wasn't a really good Christian, I didn't lead that kind of life. But He saved me. He saved me. And I am forever grateful. God gives me so many blessings that I can see now, everyday. Until that wonderful day when I walk amongst Him inside the doors of heaven, I will do His work. And I will try to live His creed. I'm opening my life to Him and just saying, "Do with me what You will." I believe that's possible for all of us, no matter what the circumstances. How great would it be, if we could all come together and realize that God is forever. He is the Way, the Truth, and the Life. Whoever believes in Him shall not perish, but have everlasting life. God forgives and saves. I'm standing here before you after everything I've been through, and I'm trying to glorify His precious name. What more proof do you need?

-And I walked back to my seat with the entire church applauding. I believe they gave me a standing ovation. That was one of the greatest moments of my new life. My new life in Christ. Now everyday is so rewarding. I can't tell you of all the blessings, there's just too many. But I feel so honored to be living for the Lord now. I was asked to give my testimony to several other churches or church groups. I've made some minor changes since the first time I wrote it (just for humor purposes), and that was it.

It's just so excellent being with Him. He's there to comfort me with my every need. And now I realize what's truly more important, in all matters. It might take me a minute, but I do get there.

I started writing this novel to mark the triumph I was going to make when I could run again. I actually first titled this book, Running Dreams. And now I've learned so much about His word that has fulfilled my life so much, more than running could ever have. It will be so great when my earthly body dies and I am sent to be with Him in Heaven forever. You too can have that luxury. Now that you know, the choice is so easy, isn't it.

"Fall & RISE"
11/13/03

(soft music intro)
"I was wasted......I thought I knew
I became broken, without a clue
Wasted dreams, shattered promises to myself
They were useless, and became the fuel—for my trip to hell...
(PAUSE)

Chorus:
But then You rescued me (music)
I can't believe I couldn't see (music)
If there's anything I can do, anything at all
To make it up to You, I'm so sorry for the fall...
(music)

I laid down for so long, for some unneeded rest
My faith was wrong, it couldn't answer for the test
So many lies, such selfishness (PAUSE/loud-)
I can't believe I put You through all this
(PAUSE)

Chorus:
But then You rescued me (music)
I can't believe I couldn't see (music)
If there's anything I can do, anything at all
To make it up to You, I'm so sorry for the fall...
(PAUSE/loud)

But You pulled me from the ashes—and gave me a new life
There will be no more false guesses
Cause now I'm in the Light…
(stay loud) I owe my life to You for helping me rise
(music briefly stops, then music solo)

End
Chorus:
You rescued me—I can't believe I couldn't see
If there's anything I can do, anything at all
To make it up to You, I'm so sorry for the fall…
(PAUSE/loud)
But You pulled me from the ashes—and gave me a new life
There will be no more false guesses
Cause now I'm in the Light…
(stay loud) I owe my life to You for helping me rise
(shortPAUSE)
You pulled me from the ashes, gave me this great life
I will never run out of chances—but I'm doing this right…
I'm in You, the beautiful Light…
I call Your name, and You're there day and night…
(PAUSE when you say)
Thank You for calling to me, "Son, rise…"
(long/soft music close)

written by:
Ryan Lee Sanders

My New Life Purpose:

My goal is Christ likeness. I know my purpose in life on earth is to do what He wills, fellowship and reach out to others for the glory of God. That is my mission, my motive, and the reason I will receive my eternal reward.